Know About Storms

by Louisa Ochoa

A big storm can make a big mess. It can wreck homes. It can knock down power lines. It can carry cars down the street.

What makes a storm BIG?
When warm air and cold air
meet, storm clouds form. The
clouds grow very dark and fill
with rain.

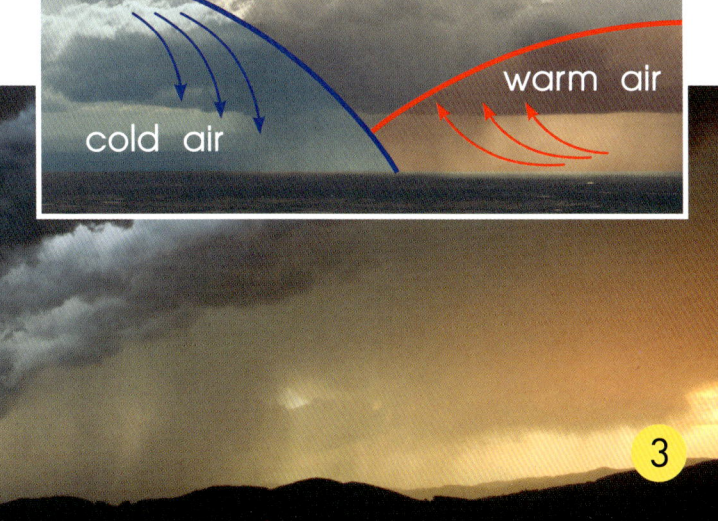

cold air

warm air

Dark clouds are a sign that a storm is near. Rain falls and wind blows. You may see lightning and hear thunder. A storm is loud!

Hail may fall, too. These sharp clumps of ice can be as big as golf balls! You can hear them hit the windows. *Ping, ping!*

Know what to do if there is a big storm. Learn what is right and wrong. You will be better off.

If you are outside, do not stand under a tree. If you are swimming, get out of the water. Wrap up in a towel and get inside.

Write a list of storm rules with a grown-up. Keep a knapsack with a flashlight, books, and games in case a big storm hits.